Who A

by

The Walkington Group

GROVE BOOKS LIMITED
Bramcote   Nottingham   NG9 3DS

CONTENTS

	Page
Introduction	3
Synopsis	4
Part 1: 'I am ...' from the human viewpoint	5
Part 2: 'I am ...' from God's viewpoint	14
Questions	23
Suggested Bible references	25

ACKNOWLEDGMENTS

We would like to thank all those friends and relations who have read our early drafts of this book, and made helpful and constructive suggestions; we would like to thank Jenny Francis who drew our cover picture for us; and we would like to thank all the fellow members of our group, who have laboured from their own individual standpoints on the different facets of our human experience.

Note: The quotation in Chapter 12 is from the poem 'High and lifted up', by Studdert Kennedy, in the collection *The Unutterable Beauty*.

First Impression May 1990
ISSN 0262-799X
ISBN 1 85174 146 1

INTRODUCTION

Have you been taught that it is wrong to think about yourself? If so, you can think again! You are important, and you are worth knowing something about, contrary to what you may have been taught; and what you know about yourself will affect your attitude to life.

You will find that this book is written from the 'I' position, and this too you may find strange for a Christian, who is expected not to be 'pushy'. But if you think about it, *we* are the only 'evidence' that we have with any certainty; it is very tempting to say, 'I know just how you feel'—you don't, only partially, and that from your own experience. So you see, I have to start from 'me'; and when I begin to understand *me,* then I can perhaps begin to understand *you.*

You will see that the book is in two parts: what 'I am' from a human viewpoint, and what 'I am' from God's viewpoint; (though rest assured that God is just as concerned with the first part as with the second). You may wish just to browse through it and think about it; or you might use it in a group, taking bits out of each section for a course of study.

The book is for anyone with an enquiring mind, who would like to know more about themself. And, while it is written with adults in mind, we hope that youngsters with an adult leader will also find it useful.

And lastly, who wrote the book and how did we do it? Quite simply, we are a bunch of people involved in ministry in the parishes of Walkington and Bishop Burton in North Humberside, (or East Yorkshire as many would like it). In the course of one of our regular meetings this book was conceived; but since then we have been through many birth-pangs together, as we each have different approaches and styles, (as no doubt you will see as you read on). However, we hope that out of our labours this little book will be a help to you.

> The Walkington Group,
> (Eve Biggs, June Brooks, John Butler, Margaret Hall,
> Linda Munt, Lucy Nicholas, Peter Jaquet, tutor,
> and Richard Burton, rector)

SYNOPSIS

PART 1: 'I am . . .' from the human viewpoint

Chapter
1. I am a living machine.
2. I am a reasoning animal.
3. I am a product of my genes.
4. I am dependent upon my environment.
5. I am male or female.
6. I am a member of a human family.
7. I am a product of my culture.
8. I am a brother or sister of the whole human race.
9. I am a person with free will.

PART 2: 'I am . . .' from God's viewpoint

Chapter
10. I am a creature of God.
11. I am not properly able to receive God's love.
12. I am enabled to receive God's love.
13. I am here for a purpose.
14. I am the hands and feet of Christ.
15. I am a member of the Church.
16. I am part of the sacramental plan of God.
17. I am truly 'me' as I am united with Christ.
18. I am destined for eternal life.

PART 1. 'I AM . . .' FROM THE HUMAN VIEWPOINT

1. I am a living machine, made up of water and living cells.

a. Fat, thin, tall, short, ugly, attractive . . . however I see myself, I am a body; and with many moving parts and organs I am a sort of living machine. As such, I can perhaps be likened to a car, a mobile machine. Part of that machine is devoted to making it function – the engine, transmission and electrics, all needing air, water, petrol and an exhaust system, and all supported by a frame and body. The other part of the machine, the wheels and steering and the human directing it, enables it to move.

b. My human machine is not unlike a car. Part of me enables me to function. I too have an engine, a transmission, a system to process the air, water and fuel my machine needs, with an exhaust system, and a skeletal frame to support the whole weight, (70% of which is water – I am in fact a walking reservoir); the whole is covered by a 'bodywork' of flesh and skin. The other part of me enables me to move and act—my arms, legs, fingers and toes and sensory organs, all directed or influenced by my brain.

c. This brain, which influences my whole human machine, both with and without conscious thought on my part, is the masterpiece of all. While infinitely slower than a computer in calculating digits and sorting and arranging facts, it is yet capable of original and constructive thought that a computer is never likely to achieve.

d. Quite unlike a car, however, my human machine will on average outlast a car many times, with normally the minimum of servicing. Where the body of a car will often wear out first, my machine's equivalent—the skin—will last a life-time, continually renewing itself; and my engine will—treated sensibly—continue beating without a break for up to 100 years. My whole machine is so wonderfully made that it can still function adequately with the loss of many parts; and increasingly it will also adapt to the replacement of spare parts. And . . . no car can reproduce itself.

e. On the one hand I am composed of merely dust and water, and on the other I am a most intricate living machine, (made up of billions of living and self-renewing cells, each of which carries my own personal 'trade mark'), which is capable of greater manual and mental skills than any other part of our known creation.

But, I am more . . .

5

2. I am a reasoning animal, a distant cousin of all the animal kingdom, but higher than them due to my developed powers of thought and speech.

a. The humble earthworm and I have a number of things in common, although somewhat unlike in both size and appearance. We both have a blood system, with a heart, (the worm has in fact five pairs); we both eat and excrete; we both have a nervous system and a brain, (though that of the worm is indeed rather smaller—the size of a pin head); we both breathe; and we both reproduce, though in decidedly different ways.

b. Such similarities with myself are to be found throughout the animal kingdom, ranging from the distant affinity with the earthworm at one end of the scale to the very close physical affinity with the primates at the other end. It is probably true that every part of my physical make-up can be paralleled with that of the great apes—though in brain size, posture, proportions, and in many details, we are clearly different.

c. With such physical affinities I also share a number of instincts with the higher animal world—such as anger and aggression, which seem to be natural accompaniments of the need for survival . . . the herd instinct, perhaps more typical of men than women . . . inquisitiveness, as part of the need to learn . . . parenting and home building . . . and the ability to think and reason, which, though less developed among the other animals, can clearly be seen, for example, in a squirrel reasoning how to reach carefully hidden food.

d. What we do not seem to share, (though it is hard to know how proven this is), is my sense of self-awareness; it is claimed that no other animal could think, 'I am . . .' Nor, of course, do any, even of the great apes, appear to have the ability for any developed powers of speech. It is this power which is a factor setting me apart from the rest of the animal world, for language enables information to be passed from generation to generation, (aided by the long dependent human childhood), and is above all the vehicle for expressing thought.

e. If the fossil record is to be believed, all of us, from the earthworm to the primates, (including me), have a common ancestry; the record seems to show that animal life, (as well as vegetable life), has evolved from the simple to the complex—either at random under natural selection, as some believe, or under a guiding force, as others hold. With such common ancestry, I am indeed genetically a cousin of the whole animal kingdom— very distant with the humbler forms of life, but far closer with such as the higher primates.

But, I am more . . .

3. I am a product of my genes, in physical appearance and race, and in many mental and emotional characteristics, and abilities.

a. I have inherited the family nose! Noses can be of real interest in our family, and it is fascinating to trace this characteristic through the generations.

b. It is fun to spot such physical characteristics, but when it comes to traits of character it is more difficult to be certain. Has my son inherited his temper from me, or has he learnt it from the struggles of being the youngest in the family?

c. Scientists have made great advances in recent years in understanding our genetic make-up. We know that certain diseases, haemophilia for example, are inherited. Work now goes on around the world to comprehend the whole human D.N.A. code.

d. My genetic make-up seems to determine to a large extent who I am. Indeed, some scientists see human beings as machine, wholly determined by their genes. If this is so, then, if I murdered somebody, surely I could not be held responsible for my action, because I was not free to do otherwise?.

e. Other scientists take a much less deterministic approach. They see genetics as painting a much broader picture of a person, leaving many details to be filled in later. So, for example, doctors now think that we can inherit a tendency to certain diseases, such as heart disease. But if I had such a tendency, by careful attention to my diet and life-style I could avert the actual illness. I may have inherited a gift for music, but only by discipline and hard work can this gift be developed. I may have inherited a bad temper, but this is no excuse; through self-discipline I can learn to control it.

f. Advances in modern genetics also bring many problems. We may soon be able to choose the sex of a baby before it is born, but should we tamper with nature in this way? Genetic engineering holds out the prospect of being able to alter some human characteristics. Would it be a good thing, say, to programme away a family propensity to depression in a child before it is born?

But, I am more . . .

4. I am dependent upon my environment, on both the vegetable and animal kingdom, often misusing my powers of thought to cause destruction beyond that caused by the rest of the animal kingdom.

a. Science has seen many successes over the past decades, but I am only just waking up to the hidden costs of those successes. I live in a culture which on the one hand can prevent London from flooding, and has harnessed the energy locked in an atom, but on the other can threaten vast areas of the world by the use of modern chemicals and the need to dispose of great volumes of toxic waste.

b. Rivers, lakes and even whole seas are threatened by this pollution, while others like the Aral Sea in Russia may run dry through poorly planned irrigation. The protective layer of ozone high in the atmosphere is patchy, while the constant production of carbon dioxide could well severely disrupt the world climate.

c. In the Third World ignorance and poverty are allowing over-grazing of much of Africa, and vast areas are in danger of becoming desert as a result. In South America, in the Amazon Basin, a combination of poverty needing timber for basic livelihood, and of greed on the part of big business, is putting what is still in fact a vast inland lake—with a phenomenal spectrum of wild life—in danger of becoming yet another dust bowl.

d. We are only just beginning to face the disastrous loss of this wild life on our planet—made up of our distant cousins which we think we can use and abuse as we like. Every year more species face extinction—from the elephants and rhinos on the plains of Africa, to the whales and dolphins in the oceans, to the birds and butterflies in our hedgerows.

e. Seen from outer space ours is a wonderful green planet, with enough food for all the teeming population—if only we could replace greed with caring responsibility for it, and if only we could realize our true place in it. As Gautama Buddha said twenty-five centuries ago, 'This world is one seamless garment', and there is no ultimate dividing line between the man, the tree and the mountain.

f. But I have proved to be a predator and a parasite; I have been living off environmental credit, and now my debts are catching up with me, 'I have reaped where I have not sown, and gathered where I have not scattered.'

But, I am more . . .

8

5. I am male or female, part masculine and part feminine, in varying degrees.

a. I am born male or female. That is to say, with very rare exceptions, I am born with male or female reproductive organs, and all the biology that goes with them. And I will be outwardly recognizable as man or woman by my physical shape and features—though these differences can be blurred by style of both hair and dress!

b. But with my *feelings* the boundaries can become more blurred—due both to genetics and to what happens to me, (even in the womb, and through early childhood and beyond). As a woman, I may exhibit some masculine feelings and attitudes, and as a man I may exhibit some feminine ones.

c. As a man, I may enjoy most the company of other men. But it may well be that I am more at home in the company of women—and this for no obviously sexual reasons. As a woman, I may like to mix with other women; but again, it may also be that I mix more happily with men.

d. As a woman, I may have the gentleness, passivity, patience and sensitivity that some would say are typical of my sex. As a man I may have the drive, aggression, impatience and less degree of sensitivity that some again would say are typical of my sex. Yet these emotional attributes can often be reversed, the woman having the aggression and the man the gentleness; and of course they can be mixed.

e. Some might say that my creative ability to write stories, paint pictures and compose music is more typically masculine than feminine. Again, some might say that my moral courage is more typically feminine, and my physical courage masculine. But these are wonderful areas for debate!

f. I may enjoy caring for the home, the family and the cooking; or I may look more to the car and the caravan, the high-fi and the video. But today so many activities are unisex, by choice as well as from necessity, and it is nearly impossible to say if any are specifically feminine or masculine; indeed, few if any can be labelled in this way. There are now even male *au pairs,* and it is not uncommon for the man to have the maternal instinct rather than the woman.

g. Whether I be a woman or a man physically, what I experience in the world of *feelings* will often not fit neatly into the accepted pattern of my male or female sex—sometimes in more extreme ways, but commonly in less obvious ways. These need not be feared or covered up or looked on with a sense of guilt, but can be recognized and welcomed as a rich part of my humanity.

But, I am more . . .

6. I am a member of a human family, and am conditioned by my family role, as a son or daughter, brother or sister, husband or wife, mother or father— often combining several roles and acting differently in each.

a. If these roles are to be truly life-giving, the members of the family will need to show to one another such attitudes as loving affection; acceptance, understanding and support; encouragement, guidance and criticism; readiness to allow for both freedom and dependence; and companionship and friendship. These can all be put under the one umbrella word of 'nurture'.

b. As a child I will need this nurture from my parents and can only learn the various meanings of it from them, primarily through my feelings rather than my intellect; and my ability to give nurture later will much depend on what I have received at this early age.

c. As a sibling I will also need this nurture from my brothers and sisters. But if I am one of the older ones, I may have a new role thrust upon me, by having to provide such nurture to those younger than me. This can 'stretch' me and help me mature; but it can also 'over-stretch' me and damage me.

d. As a spouse I will need both to give nurture and receive it, if the marriage is to be a good one, (with an adult equal relationship). But there will be times when, for reasons such as illness, tiredness or crisis, I will feel 'fragile' and like a child, and will need to receive nurture from my spouse in the role of a parent. As a spouse then I may be both a child and a parent, as well as an equal adult.

e. As a parent I will need to give nurture to my children, and will continue to do this in varying degrees even when they have left the nest; and they may always be the 'kids' to me. Likewise, I may always be a child to my own parents, and may often *feel* like a child when I am with them. And in my old age I may increasingly be a child to my own children, as I become dependent on them for nurturing.

f. Thus I will often be, *and feel,* a child, parent or an equal in the same family, depending on whom I am with at the time, *and upon what is expected from me.* All these roles will often produce conflicts of allegiance; and all may feel forced into roles that I might not otherwise freely choose.

But, I am more . . .

10

7. I am a product of my culture, my up-bringing, my parents and family, (nuclear and extended), my race, my society, my friends and my religion.

a. 'My mother always said . . . my sister used to . . . I saw on the box . . . blacks always . . . I blame the unions for . . . the bosses never . . . none of the kids at school . . . what would my friends say if . . . as a Christian (Muslim, Jew, Hindu), I wouldn't . . .' I am subtly or grossly influenced by what is said and done to me, both past and present; this begins in childhood, and will continue from friend and foe alike until I die.

b. During my childhood, my family will have the most formative influence on me, and will leave their stamp on my character—for good or ill—for the rest of my life. A secure and happy childhood will leave me a secure and outgoing person, while the reverse can leave me insecure, anxious and introverted. With my peers at school, and later with my friends at work, there will be safety and pleasure in 'fitting in'; and it can be painful to fail to fit in with, or break out from, what they think and do.

c. Class distinctions are a further confused influence, as today they can arise less from accidents of birth than from such an un-reasoning and emotional attitude as disdain . . . for those with less or more money than me . . . for the exploiting bosses or greedy workers . . . for those backing another political party . . . for those using private or public education or health care . . . for those with 'posh' or 'rough' accents . . . for those enjoying macho sports or less obviously masculine ones.

d. Nothing in my society assails me so much as the media. Through my letter-box and into my living room come reports and pictures of violence and hate, jealousy and greed, as well as peace-making, generosity and kindness, and also views both potted and biased as well as balanced and informed. I cannot avoid their influence.

e. If I have a religious belief, be it Christian, Jewish, Muslim or Hindu, be it liberal or strict, my character and culture will weave a subtle pattern with it. Most of us are born into the faith we hold, and our culture will do much to seek to modify it; my own character and experience will also bear upon the 'brand' I choose. But once I am committed to my faith, my thoughts and actions cannot avoid being deeply influenced by it.

f. John Donne in the seventeenth century said, 'No man is an island'. Indeed, I am part of a veritable crowd of people and events.

But, I am more . . .

8. I am a brother or sister of the whole human race, with all the responsibilities of that relationship; and I only begin to be truly human when I accept those responsibilities.

a. When I was a child, I would play with a child . . . of any race, class or colour and not even realize that such things existed. There were no barriers—even that of language could be surmounted. But now that I am a man (or woman) I have put away such childish things as trust and sharing, and put on such adult things as fear and selfishness. As a child I instinctively knew brother and sisterhood beyond my human family; as an adult such natural instinct seems dulled if not lost.

b. It is true that among the starving and homeless in our society, and in much of the third world, there may often be a brother and sisterhood 'in adversity'. But for me in my comfortable culture any brother or sisterhood beyond my family is restricted to my close circle of friends, my club, my local church, my union or professional body. Beyond these horizons, knowingly or unknowingly, I will tend to exploit rather than support.

c. In Britain I am part of the world economic élite. I live in a luxury unimaginable to most of the world, with my wealth dependent upon the poverty of others. I can buy relatively cheap basic commodities such as tea, tin, coffee and oil, because my culture dominates the markets and dictates prices.

d. I live in a shrinking world, where—due to the speed of communication—the other side of the world is only a moment away; what I do in my corner affects people thousands of miles away. Cultures different from mine have been destroyed and their people left with only my cultural model to aspire to. Yet I am not prepared to afford the environmental consequences of anyone sharing my life-style.

e. The more I have, the less my potential for solidarity with humans the world over is realized; fear for the loss of what I have, coupled with a lack of readiness to share, diminishes me. I only truly begin to be human when I accept the privileges and responsibilities of brotherhood and sisterhood with others around the world—for this opens the way for trust, compassion and sharing.

f. Whether I like it or not, I *am* related to the rest of the human race. Genetically, they are my most extended family, and they call upon me to recognize this and act on it.

But, I am more . . .

9. I am a person with free will, however limited and determined by all the above attributes; and it is this free will which partly makes me 'me'.

a. To do or not to do, that is the question. Choices, choices, decisions, decisions, life is full of them. From the moment I wake, when I have to choose between ten minutes more in bed and a rushed breakfast, or less comfort now and more later . . . to deciding whether to drive or bus . . . to write this letter or that . . . to drink or not . . . to garden or take the family out . . . to marry the boy or not . . . to have a baby or not . . . to buy this house or that . . . you name it, every moment of my life I am faced with choices large and small.

b. And how I decide will be affected by all the factors touched on so far in this book. My physical make-up can cause me to be lively or sluggish . . . my power of thought can be both an asset and a liability . . . my forebears will influence me . . . I cannot escape the effect of rain and sun, heat and cold . . . as a male or female I will think and feel differently . . . family allegiances and my place in the pecking order press on me . . . my up-bringing, my culture and my religion help to form my thinking and feeling . . . and my comparative affluence or my poverty will affect me almost more than anything else.

c. And yet . . . and yet . . . to mug or not to mug, to help or not to help . . . to steal or not to steal, to give or not to give . . . to terrorize or not to terrorize, to care or not to care . . . to rape or not to rape, to love or not to love . . . am I a machine or a free agent? If I am brought up in a background of crime, will I inevitably turn to crime? If I am brought up in a happy, loving, caring and balanced home, will I inevitably live a life of honesty and caring?

d. There would seem to be enough evidence that I *can* turn from a life of crime, as well as from drink and drugs; while there is all too much evidence that I can turn *to* such a life from a 'good' background. It seems that I do not have a mechanistic make-up, that I do have this strange indefinable attribute of free will, (however limited by my inner influences), enabling me to rise above these influences, and to do what *I* want and deep down believe to be good.

e. Humanly speaking, I am a complex mixture of attributes from the past and present, physical and emotional. These are, if you like, my 'data' with which I start. Partly what makes me 'me' as a unique individual is the way I deal with those data with my free will.

BUT, I am much, much more . . .

13

PART 2. 'I AM . . .' FROM GOD'S VIEWPOINT

10. I am a creature of God, with this in common with the whole created universe; and with that universe I belong to God, and through it I am blessed by God.

a. Behind the person that I am lies a host of creative elements—my environment and my culture, my forebears and my up-bringing, and the exercising of my free will. But . . . behind all this again, and working through all this, lies that mysterious being that we call God—who is both the creator and centre of my being and of all the world around me, and who reaches out to me in love through his creation.

b. Thus, while a free agent, I am yet a created being and an integral part of God's creation; I am part of a divine plan, into which both I and the visible and invisible world around me are created to fit.

c. This creation of God, this world, this universe, is 'good' in the sense of pleasing to God rather than kindly to man. It is beautiful, but not always gentle—in fact it is often dangerous, as I can know to my cost; anything big can be dangerous by virtue of its very size—a gentle cart-horse can be dangerous if it steps by accident on my foot, and I have seen or felt a gentle wind or sea turn into a gale or terrifying breakers.

d. This creation, while potentially dangerous, is also a life-enhancing setting for me. I am blessed through it by God—who is revealed as both majestic and dangerous, and yet beautiful, loving and kindly. And with this same creation I also belong to God. Like the creation around me, I am intended to function properly when in harmony with my Creator; and the creation can teach me much on this score.

e. I am made in the image of my Creator; and one aspect of this fact is that I too am meant to be a creator. I am not intended to sit on the side-lines, just watching and waiting for things to happen. Whether it be through the creative arts, or by carpentry or gardening, cooking or teaching, manufacturing of planning, carrying out scientific research or exploration, healing the body and mind or conquering personal handicap, giving birth to life or nurturing a family, or 'just' praying . . . I am sharing in the work of the One who made me. And if *my* creations are life-enhancing, I will be growing more like my Creator.

But, I am more . . .

11. I am not properly able to receive this blessing, this love of God, through ignorance and fear, and through the misuse of my free will.

a. I am not properly able to receive God's love, through ignorance and fear, through weakness and the deliberate misuse of my free will. At times I feel that I can do without God, and at times I feel like a little pawn in a much more powerful game.

b. Chaos and evil and destructive forces seem to be all around me. Scientists tell us that the universe is tending towards chaos; the animal kingdom strives onwards with apparently great cruelty and savagery, and much in the world looks unjust. Why must children die of leukaemia, and good and honest men die of cancer before they are old? It can seem as if there is a cancer in the universe itself.

c. I do see reflections of God's love all around me—in forgiveness and mercy and gentleness. But even when I aspire to this love, it eludes me; the love I show to others is shallow and selfish. At times I despise myself.

d. God in his love touches my life, but then my shame seems so much greater, and the struggles with myself so much stronger. I grasp at love by imposing my own rules on my life, but these rules only work eventually to dominate my life.

e. My failure to receive God's love has a destructive effect in my life. Some of these destructive results are described in earlier chapters of our study. My sexuality can be a destructive force, my family roles are mixed-up and obscure. I need other people, but I also strive to be better than them; I need the world in which I live, but my life-style can be destructive of the environment.

f. Who can liberate my life so that I can receive God's love? And who can enable me to love as I have been loved?

But, I am more . . .

15

12. I am enabled to receive God's blessing and love, by the power and love of Christ, through his life, death and resurrection.

a. I am a unique and very special person, moulded and loved by the Creator. He offers to me a loving relationship, but I am not properly able to receive it. I am like a hamster locked in its cage with little knowledge of life outside my cage and no idea how to find that life. Maybe I feel safer in my cage!

b. I also see that I live in a broken world of war and greed. How can I make sense of this broken world? And how can this broken world discover healing and love?

c. Christians have always seen that the key to healing for our broken world, and the healing of my relationship with God, lies in Jesus' life and death. Jesus enters our broken world in love. Here is a vision of Jesus' healing love that one padre brought to the troops in the trenches in the first world war:
'God, the God I love and worship, reigns in sorrow on the Tree,
Broken, bleeding, but unconquered, very God of God to me . . .
And above all in the horror of the cruel death He died,
Thou hast bid us seek Thy glory, in a criminal crucified.
And we find it—for Thy glory is the glory of Love's loss,
And Thou hast no other splendour but the splendour of the Cross.'

d. Now I see that Jesus offers me the promise of a loving encounter with God, and a way of making sense of this broken world. Christ has entered into my world and has opened a way to a new communion with God. With his unconditional, vulnerable love, Jesus cuts through my pretence and the false images I have of myself, and restores to me my true humanity. And with his creative unconquered love Jesus reaches out to the world to bring healing where before there was greed and hate. Traditionally, the Christian faith has seen this poor man's death as having eternal significance for the universe; are Christians still able to say this today in the light of our greater understanding of the universe?

e. When the first disciples looked back on the crucifixion after the resurrection, they began to interpret Jesus' death with ideas such as sacrifice, redemption and salvation. But these Biblical concepts must become more than just ideas for me. Encountering the healing love of God is the joy of the Christian's life.

f. For me, encountering Jesus has meant a new sense of God's love, a growing acceptance of myself and others, a release from guilt and anxiety, a new joy and hope, a growing understanding of myself, which has led to a more accepting understanding of others and a more realistic concern for the world.

But, I am more . . .

16

13. I am here for a purpose, where this life can be seen as a community setting, in which I can learn to be fully human—within the love of God and the blessings of his world; and it is this purpose that gives me hope.

a. 'What am I here for? What are we doing here?' These are questions that countless people have asked. Perhaps the answer lies in looking on this life as a school—not, that is, as a place to earn marks and pass exams, or even as a place where I can learn to be good, but rather as a community setting in which I can begin to learn to be fully human.

b. This I saw earlier, in my need to accept the privilege of relating to my fellow humans. But now I see that it involves more—my learning to experience, in the midst of this 'school of life', the presence of God, with his love, forgiveness, guidance, joy, sorrow and compassion. And so it seems that he intends me to experience his presence in the context of this physical world—not in spite of it or removed from it, but *through it.* I am to learn to know him through its beauties and glories, its storms and calms; through its loves and hatreds, its sins and forgiveness; through its joys and sorrows, its poverty and riches.

c. If I try to take a short cut to God, and shun what this world has to offer, it will be like learning my lessons at school and shunning the community life of the school; I will be only half a person or less. I will have avoided the physical and emotional pleasures and pains of companionship, the challenges, excitements and frustrations of working with others, the opportunities for fun and adventure, the experience of competition, failure and achievement. My sensitivity, understanding and compassion will be undeveloped, and my experience of life narrow.

d. I now come to see that all these experiences go towards the creation and building up of the essential 'me'; and, what is supremely important, *that God is to be encountered in them all.* I see that he and I communicate not just in the silent moments, but also in the turmoil of relationships and activity, in the unspoken feelings of joy, sorrow, pain or despair, and in the mental wrestling with problems.

e. This school of life can be a hard school—much harder than many of those schools of our youth, where we did not necessarily spend the happiest days of our lives! Yet, while joy and excitement can reveal to me some of the essential nature of God, so also hard slogging, adversity and pain can—if I will allow them—both build up my character and throw me more surely into the loving arms of God.

But, I am more . . .

17

14. I am the hands and feet of Christ, on whom he depends to do his work, guided and inspired, (whether I know it or not), by his Holy Spirit.

a. The Bible leaves me in no doubt that as a Christian I am expected to show practical concern for the needs of others. 'Whatever you do not do for others', says Jesus, 'you do not do for me.' Yet I often search for my role in the Christian community, wondering what special job God has planned for me; or I think of the immense demands of the world, and my attitudes become negative. I begin to wonder what one person can do in a world of so much suffering.

b. Perhaps the starting point is to begin to look at the problems through different eyes, to see what I can do in positive terms rather than being bogged down by what I cannot achieve. Jesus himself chose to live his life among the poor of Galilee, healing the sick and feeding the hungry. For many others now, like Mother Teresa of Calcutta and Brother Roger of Taizé, this life-style is a reality.

c. But mostly this world is made up of millions of ordinary people like me, on whom the fate of millions of others depends. For many around me my greatest gift is my time. Those grieving the death of a loved one . . . the victim of a broken marriage . . . those depressed, for whom life has no meaning . . . those who are lonely or ill . . . all these need a sensitive and sympathetic listener, who might even replace a life-time of drugs. Others need more practical care . . . a baby sitter or someone to do the shopping . . . a fruit cake or a meal on the table . . . these can show in a new and dramatic way that God really cares.

d. God does not leave me alone in this. His Holy Spirit works in every aspect of my life, and guides, prompts, challenges and empowers me in all that I do and am. Through prayer I become more receptive and open to him, as he changes me into Christ's likeness. It is he who gives me patience, tolerance and strength to serve others for his sake.

e. But some things seem totally beyond me. The appalling plight of millions in the Third World comes to me through the media, leaving me with a sense of overwhelming inadequacy. Jesus knew that not even a sparrow falls to the ground without God knowing; perhaps then, my concern should be for that one sparrow, of infinite worth to God. In fact, this may mean sponsoring a poor child or giving regularly to a relief agency; and praying for the poor as Jesus prays for me.

f. It is said that the mark of a Christian is 'one who cares'. I need not search for my role in society. The world in which God has placed me, and which is for so many a nightmare, creates for me a world of opportunities to become the hands and feet of Christ.

But, I am more . . .

15. I am a member of the Church, the great family to which all brothers and sisters of Christ belong by their baptism.

a. If I refer to the church, I might be thinking of a building, perhaps standing attractively above the village, charming but irrelevant to the modern world, or maybe looking tawdry and half abandoned in a 'down and out' city suburb.

b. What a false impression of the significance of Christ's Church this would be! In truth the Church is a great body of people, a People of God, responding to Christ's call. We are on a pilgrimage of life, instruments of God's transforming power in this world, and moving towards a time of unimaginable glory when his creation will be completed. I am a member of that army for whom victory is already assured!

c. In baptism I become a member of the Church, a new person, forgiven for my pride, my shortcomings and failings—my sins—accepting Jesus as my Lord. The Holy Spirit comes upon me to enable me to be a worker for Christ, a member of his Church, a friend of God and a fighter against evil. The Holy Spirit strengthens me to overcome the self-centred desires in my life. 'No matter where I happen to be, by prayer I can set up an altar to God in my heart.' (St. John Chrysostom)

d. The Holy Spirit dwells in the Church and makes it a living reality, and not a mere worldly organization. As a member I am committed to the worship of the Church, and especially to receive the sacrament of Holy Communion, by which we are united with Christ.

e. I become a brother or sister in Christ, not just of those in 'my' congregation or in 'my' particular denomination, but of all Christians wherever they are in the world, be they young or old, whatever their condition, race or colour. My fellowship with them calls on me to support the Church in prayer and action, in Christ's mission.

f. It is easy to overlook or not take seriously 'all those who rejoice with us but on another shore, and in a greater light, that multitude which no man can number.' This is the invisible Church, the Church triumphant. If I do believe the Gospel message, I believe that death has been trampled down by Christ's death on the Cross, freely given for us, and by his resurrection. When we praise God and pray, do we not join the unceasing praise and prayers of all who have 'run the race' and 'fought the good fight'? My faith should include the invisible part of the Church, since my faith is connected to the question of the continuity of life beyond the grave.

But, I am more . . .

16. I am part of the sacramental plan of God, where God reveals himself through his physical creation—the universe, this world and human beings, but supremely through Jesus Christ and his sacraments.

a. Many things in the world around me draw me closer to God. Through them God speaks to me, helping me to understand his love and purpose for me more clearly.

b. I remember on holiday one summer, walking out in the evening when the children were asleep, and watching the sun over the loch and the distant mountains. The still evening air and beautiful views seemed to draw me closer to God, and helped me to put my hectic life into God's perspective.

c. Jesus found being alone and surrounded by the grandeur of nature helped him to pray and focus his ministry. We often read of Jesus walking by the lakeside or in the mountains in prayer.

d. I can well describe the world around me as sacramental. The world was made by God and it is part of his self-expression. Every part of God's creation has the potential to become a medium through which God can speak to me. In creation I can encounter God.

e. I can also encounter God through the everyday acts of love shown to me by others. A touch, a kiss, a letter from a friend, a dozen jam tarts baked for a friend, can all be sacramental.

f. My most profound encounters with God are through Christ; in him and through him all the heights and depths of my life can be sacramental. Reflecting on his life, death and resurrection draws me to the heart of God. His life and death help me to make sense of my life. My weakness, failure and vulnerability are a sharing with Christ in his death. This acceptance of my life in God leads me to discover love, joy and hope, which are a sharing in Christ's resurrection. Thus my experience is mirrored in Christ's experience, and life's depths and heights can themselves open a channel to God.

g. I also meet with Christ in the sacraments he gave us. Baptism itself mirrors Easter in the symbolism of death and resurrection. And the eucharist is historically linked with the passion. Communion for me is always the most profound act of worship; it cannot be superficial. The bread and wine, part of the created world, draw me to the Last Supper and to Christ's death; and through them God's love, forgiveness and new life 'reach those parts other things cannot reach'—and also link me to my fellow-Christians wherever they may be.

But, I am still more . . .

17. I am only truly 'me' as I become united with Christ—and with other Christians; for he is the vine and we are the branches; and the vine is made up *only* of branches, each one growing from another.

a. Today's world is a battle-ground. I may fight to survive the effects of war, famine, grief or illness, or I may suffer the deep pain of rejection as a child or partner of a broken marriage. I might be one who suffers at the hands of the assertive and confident businessman who is determined to get to the top, or one whose confidence was shattered by the constant belittling of a parent or teacher who measured my world in terms of my intellect.

b. I carry with me all sorts of thoughts and memories which have shaped my whole life. These may have left me with a feeling of worthlessness in the eyes of others, or a sense of superiority over others. The way I see myself determines all my thoughts and actions. I am not governed by who I am, but by who I think I am; and this view of myself colours all my life.

c. Christ's intention for me is to see myself truthfully. His love for me helps me to accept this truth. And his acceptance and forgiveness set me free from the past, give me joy in discovering and becoming truly myself, as I accept myself as I really am. As Christ's love reaches out to me, I begin to surrender my life to him and grow in loving dependence on him. The knowledge of his love gives me back my self-worth, and gives me a deep sense of security. Prayer is one special way that helps me to receive his love.

d. The picture Jesus gives of himself as the vine helps me to understand my relationship to him and to others. It reminds me that the vine is only made up of branches, and that through these the love of God is mediated one to another. True life and understanding of myself come through my dependence upon the vine, and self worth is restored when I stay in his love, united to him as a branch is united to the vine. But only by living in community with other branches, giving and accepting love, can I become truly myself.

e. My new acceptance of myself helps me to relate to others without trying constantly to prove myself. Understanding and accepting the conflicting feelings within me give me insight into some of the pain and struggles of others. This helps me to relate to others and others to me, and these new relationships can in turn be healing for me. Understanding others gives me a starting point to guide others to the healing of Christ.

And finally, and most wonderfully . . .

18. I am destined for eternal life, where this life is not an end but a beginning, preparing us for the Greater Life Beyond, with God and all the saints, who watch over us now.

a. 'Is there a life beyond this one? Where am I going, if anywhere?' These are questions which must have bugged human beings from the beginning of time. And indeed, what lies before me after this present 'school of life' is far less known than what lies before a youngster leaving a human school.

b. And yet . . . if I believe in a God of love, there are certain things that I have a right to believe. For starters, I have a right to believe that the love of God cannot be less than that of a good and loving parent, and will indeed be immeasurably greater.

c. I thus have a right to believe that this life is not an end but a beginning, that there will be a greater life beyond this one. For what loving parents, having let their child help for several days to prepare for his or her own party, with all the fun and frustrations, would then say, 'There's to be no party, we've only been pretending.'?

d. Indeed, Jesus confirms this reasoning, both by his resurrection, and also by what he said. 'Today you will be with me in Paradise . . . In my Father's house there are many mansions . . . God is not the God of the dead, but of the living.'

e. Further, with such a loving God as revealed by Jesus, I may presume to trust that I will be accepted as I am, and not rejected—however bad I may be or feel to be, and that the only barriers between me and God are the ones I erect. I expect to be faced with the truth of what I am and what I have been, but it will all be in love.

f. And I will still be me, with my own identity, growing in love as I grow closer to God, or awakening into the glory of God's loving presence. But not just me! As here, but far, far more, there will be countless others, known to us and un-known, the great cloud of witnesses referred to in the Epistle to the Hebrews. And of course we'll recognize those we've known and loved—in God's own way; what a dreadful cosmic joke it would be were it to be otherwise.

g. And then . . . who knows? Brighter, more glorious, more lovely and more loving, it will surely be better and more wonderful than you or I can ever imagine.

QUESTIONS

Chapter

1 a. Do you think there is a limit to spare-part surgery?
b. What parts of your body, if any, do you dislike? If so, why?
c. Do you worry about your body breaking down?
d. How far should life-support systems be used? When is a person really dead?

2 a. Do you think it is right to use animals for medical research?
b. One of the causes of man's rise to power in the animal world is his adaptability; how adaptable are you to change?
c. How does it feel to you to be related to all the animal world? Or do you reject such a belief?

3 a. What do you feel are the good and the bad characteristics that you have inherited?
b. If scientists could change just one of your characteristics, physical or emotional, which would you change?

4 a. Is there anything politically you can do to tackle some of these economic and environmental problems?
b. Is there any way you can simplify your life-style, and would it be of any value anyway?
c. As we are all dependent on our environment, is it more important to give to that or to people?

5 a. What is your attitude to homosexuals and lesbians?
b. Men are prone to the herd instinct; women prefer a 'best friend'; do you agree?
c. Do you think men are afraid of women?

6 a. In what ways do you think an older sibling can be over-stretched in caring for the younger ones?
b. How big is the role of parent or child in your adult life?
c. How successfully have you coped with ties of dependence?
d. What conflicts of allegiance can you see in your family?

7 a. Can you complete some of the phrases in para a. from your own experience?
b. What were some of the most formative experiences in your childhood and time at school?
c. What part does your culture play in the practising of your religion?

8 a. How can you extend brotherhood and sisterhood without condescension?
b. How would you feel if your local school had 80% children of a different culture?
c. When did you last attend a church outside your own community, (other than for a baptism, wedding or funeral)?

Chapter

9 a. Is free will only limited to humans? (Have you ever tried to drive a sheep through a hole in a hedge?!)
  b. What would you say to someone who said, 'I had no choice ...'?
  c. Do you believe in horoscopes? If so, how do they fit in with free will?
  d. Do you sometimes feel powerless when circumstances seem to allow you no real choices in life?

10 a. Do you see death as a natural part of creation, or as a result or punishment of human sin?
  b. How far do you think we can know God through the natural creation?
  c. What parts of the creation do you find specially life-enhancing?

11 a. Is there a cancer within our universe, and if so, where do you see its symptoms, and what are its roots?
  b. What stops you loving yourself?

12 a. Rewrite the list in para. f. in your own words.
  b. Explain from your own experience the verses 2 Cor. 5.21 and 3.18.
  c. How do you understand the Biblical concepts in para. e.?

13 a. Which of the important experiences of life do you feel you have missed out on? Can you do anything about it?
  b. Can you identify any 'pairs' in para. b. which have affected your life?
  c. How far does the second part of para. d. fit in with your beliefs and experience of prayer?

14 a. Is service to the community really service to God, even if the motive is not consciously religious?
  b. Was Jesus doing the will of God more perfectly when he was teaching and healing than when he was a carpenter? Has the answer a bearing on our job?
  c. St. Francis says that in giving we receive. In what ways have you experienced this?

15 a. Do all members of my own congregation seem to be my brothers and sisters? What are my attitudes to our failings?
  b. Do I feel uneasy or suspicious of Christians from other denominations? How would I react to a Friends' meeting, an Evangelical service or an Orthodox Liturgy?
  c. Could I attend a service at a church where many members were still in favour of apartheid?

16 a. Describe times when God has spoken to you through the created world.
  b. What times of struggle and pain have drawn you closer to God?
  c. How have the sacraments of baptism and communion helped you?